COUNTRY

Country Music

WILL BURNS

First published in 2020
by Offord Road Books

offordroadbooks.co.uk
@OffordRoadBooks

Typeset by Offord Road Books
Printed in the UK by TJ International

ISBN 978–1–916–01591–3

1 3 5 7 9 10 8 6 4 2

O•R•B

for Nina

Contents

Or he may learn that stones themselves may speak
Flintly their language of heartbreak.

Malcolm Lowry, *Injured Stones*

COUNTRY MUSIC

Country

This is the mid country.
The hill country.
It is the rain country,
kite country, slow country.
Some call it
cloud country
or lightning country.
I have heard it called
the nether country,
Buck's country
and thieves' country.
We were warned
that it was punch
up and fruitcake
                    country.

It was built of bone
and sold off in car boot
fields, piece by piece.

Drive South Listening to Country Music

(for Greg Burns)

Twenty miles from the trout farm
there is just music

and the green Volvo and the clouds
breaking open now

where it had been
raining hard.

I'm wishing it was a whole
continent we had to travel into,

with drives that last
whole days to get to the water,

and big game fish and names
like sockeye and wahoo to learn –

a land ready to receive us,
right to the edge of the mesa.

But happy enough too
with our worn hills

of hacked up chalk,
driving half an hour with you, the quiet brother,

and the pedal steel flowing
into your silence like all your best fish.

A Summer Blues

The blue wall. And the house
holding here like a bur
in the shade of Shiver Hill.
The begging and begging
for you to build again – this time
something cool and that will last
and high up in the trees.

But you aren't the man
you appeared to be
that first night on Prospect Street.

So the hard mornings–after.
Mornings of frying eggs
in a skillet, spitting oil against
the wall, blue as a chalkhill blue.
A crust of ladybirds inked
dead in the kitchen window
and guitar strings
that might rust to blue or ring forever.

And my nights like a praying drunk –
smashed and alone and falling asleep
watching YouTube clips
of catfish rising and taking
pigeons, teal, a dog even
off the water's broken surface.
This kind of deep dark is all I will ever earn.

Thirteen

The train stations of middle England
with their 'Parkway' epithets,
fried breakfasts and untidy homeliness.
A couple of buzzards, farmland.
Almost nothing to see.
I notice a certain harmony
for the first time on an old song.
Something I must have been missing
for years – as if it had never been.
I wonder what it would feel like
to talk to you once more about that small noise –
that near inaudible voice.

Cycnus in Soho

We met up again in that old, central clot of London.
It suited you – its secret knowledge,
danger, certain hedonistic qualities – that edge
which had not yet had its keenness dulled, its end begun.

Then we had our place full of roll-up ash
and would-be artists, where I found you most mornings,
a foot from the television, watching *Friends*.
A trash of pizza boxes, beer bottles, cash.

You moved in when your old house burned down.
No fault of your own, no blame attached, and yet no plan.
But a little money, so you cut your ties and ran.
A bag of clothes, some books, a taxi across town.

The nights became cheap. For me at least – in that sense I
    was shabby.
Would you consider all this an outrageously late
attempt (I've gone about it somewhat stagily, I admit that
    at any rate)
to pay back what I owe? Would you indulge, again, what
    must have then been pity?

At school you had a bit of Rupert Brooke
and more yet of the Californian anti-hero –
plain white T-shirt, or grey marl, the first to have a mobile
    phone.
That battered old Ford Fiesta that *just* undermined your
    looks.

The phone. Remember when it went off in History
and you answered (didn't you?)? Even Sir was leering,
the class all ears, and you just said, 'Hey. What are *you*
    wearing?'
You wore your intellect as one-liners, elegantly, effortlessly.

There was rage behind the cool stand-offishness –
a parade of broken safety doors (the damage paid), the
    unease
of so many later friends and their 'please . . . take him
    home' pleas.
The dinner-party classic of that French arrest.

I am trying to think (don't waste your time, you would say,
    it hurts too much
to see you struggling to keep up) if it was some kind of
    disgust
that you felt towards my, what was it in the end . . . lust?
It is true that it was always me that chased, or more banal,
    tried to get in touch.

It took a Herculean will
to stop beating myself on your approval.
But I did stop bringing my bullshit to your door, or your
    altar, after all.
Left you in a seaside town softening your brain with pills.

The seasons have long abandoned all meaningful
relationships (or oppositions) to one another.
They are interchangeable, a pair of badly-plotted twin
    brothers.
I sometimes wonder after all

if I didn't make you up entirely.
Because who is the protagonist here in the end –
me, or those fine looks, to which all youth must attend?
The agony, finally, is *not* changing. Never changing,
   oh, the agony.

Seersucker

The seersucker suit turns down a drink.
Though I have seen him drinking wine before.
Chicken and onions, talk of his Soho . . . receding,
    recessions.
It's a plain dinner we receive, but good all the same.

Kindness, I Suppose

(for Adam Killip, John-George Cooper & Steve Blackwell)

The days pitched from morning
straight into the nights,
days of vodka-7s in the shower,
and you bringing over the first good guitar
any of us owned and playing all day –
broken songs from another continent
we couldn't have understood,
steel strung and sung in high harmony.

Memories in plaid
now lost to the shock of us all grown old.
The present is corduroy (and in your case works out).
I barely remember a chord, let alone the words.
The house on the green has since burned down –
just like the bar on the Holloway Road.
Our hero was Townes Van Zandt.
Still dead, I assume?
He played his last show
to a half-empty Borderline (and that's now closed) –
out of kindness I suppose.

Transmission

Remembering there is
provenance to the curved
ditch that runs below the trees

at the foot of the hill.
Something about when
and why it was made –

a name, however dimly offered.
He can see it from here,
from his back window.

He understands this place
like a painter would. Thinks
what are the broad bands of hundreds

of shades of green? Of information?
What are these pylons or the high speed
through the tamed and thewy earth?

He watches it rain after dinner.
Tired, he sits and picks bits
from between his teeth.

And he watches it rain
all the next day too, sitting
in his cousin's motor spares shop,

or standing on the forecourt,
cleaning his blackened nails
right back to the quick.

My Grandmother Arrives in the Home Counties

I

To wind up here of all places,
sometime after the war –
a fighter pilot husband from the base
on Hong Kong killed in a car crash
on leave. Widowed, comatose,
and suddenly, unexpectedly, foreign.
My mother talks of what she wore.
Sunglasses, pelts – a wardrobe
from a non-existent time, or home.
Those who suffer movement
see something of the world
at least. Some welcome
or unwelcome or indifferent port.

II

The falsehood is that there is little
left for us to know.
More likely, more truthful,
is that things of hers got lost
in the gap between their languages.
My mother's council estate English,
her mother's Spanish and Portuguese –
by way of Peru, Porto, the devil-knows-where.
There were times it did not matter,
my mother has always said,

she would not speak for days on end.
A four-foot-ten vessel for her own *saudade*.
Inscrutable. One way or another
too much for two husbands
and this strange, unremarkable
little town where I keep my trap
shut now, when the talk turns
to Europe.

III

I was young when she died.
As a point of fact
she moves further and further away
from those of us remaining.
Hotel names, ledgers touching
on an early life she tried to hide.
The sap of the stone pine.
The prickle of a praying mantis
on my pale and childish hand.
All to be denied even as they fade.
It is not recall of her
that comes to me now in airports
or those big European train depots,
but an imagining.
Bad choices piling up like debts.

Bastard Service

The unit of violence in these hills
is no longer the disused MOD site
but the bloody mess of individuals –
plastic stuff outside an abandoned tent,
tobacco packaging, two newspapers
(detail – the recent spate of one-on-one
chemical attacks), small bags of dog shit.
Of course we got lost, looking, carelessly,
for a certain kind of tree, a crossed
whitebeam and mountain ash. You headed home
at some point, done in. Alone, I made camp,
marked up the point of separation
on a map, and thought over and over
of the phrase – *leave no trace, leave no trace.*

True Service

Bare fields along the ridge. Pale soil
and crows in the gardens, crows and rain.
Mushrooms growing through the lawns,
their essive case a spreading beneath
all other things – the flower beds, the trees,
the outdoor furniture (rusted, ruined . . .).
In this place I am no where, no body,
nothing but the one who picked the big dog
fox off the road the night before, run-down,
his breath a bubble of blood against my arm,
and lowered him onto the shining grass.
His side heaved, then stopped, and thank God,
the animal died before I could worry
what I would need to do next.

Wild Service

Late July. Dragonfly days like fat,
when the river played itself
in halftime, air so thick it had killed birdsong.
I lost the river path, lay on my back
under a wild service tree.
I could feel there would be thunder,
on its given day, that would mean
no more than domestic grief and headaches –
broken bricks and roof tiles, shattered timber.
We were hundreds of miles apart
and despite my holding onto some dull hope,
as stilled and desperate as the stream itself,
I suppose you decided in the end
that it was just too far for you to come.

The Light

You turn the light on
when you come
in the room.
Honestly,
it's as simple as that.

Guy

Strange, that time of year
when the maybugs come hard
and thick and inky.
See them in the windows

of the White Horse Hotel
where they congregate
or in the kerbside dirt
where they are groggy and dying.

To feel the evening coming up
and to stream one way or another,
down the streets lined
with hornbeam and dog shit

and then at once to feel
all these things change. Down
to the angles of the earth itself, the nature
of your work and all other men.

To feel all that was once certain cut
and run under the folding steel,
like garden birds that scatter
from a bird of prey.

For the Birds

The hawks struggle on in the wind.
They are a regality of sorts
despite our knowledge that they feed
from landfill these days, like gulls.
Other birds have given up entirely.
The geese, for instance, seem easy
at finding themselves in this shabby backwater
with its improbable claims
to once owning half the map.
The tick-list has become wishful,
or worse perhaps – something like a tic.

A Chinese Restaurant
Called Happiness

The first time we met you asked how
I'd be spending the night –
a couple of Coronas, Lowry and Calexico
if I remember it right . . .
that book – or was it a life? – of letters, poems, fragments.

You let yourself out in increments.
Best-liked Chinese dish here (sweet and sour prawns?),
a painter there (Chris Ofili and was it Wassily Kandinsky?).
The Beatles (*White Album*, George, your mother's city).

We stopped talking one day
but we weren't really talking by that stage anyway.
Just pitting messages against one another.
A channel between us and everything meagre, everything
    scrap
where you wanted honest fodder.

The one time I flew over to visit
I looked out of the window for the whole flight.
Imagined all the living being done unseen, implicit,
in each minuscule, framed, portion of sea.

Fish Market in Normandy

By god they could talk about the past,
as if it were a waste of time to be there when we were.
I sleepwalked along –
the interloper from a different history,
the man whose name was wrong.
Your father stopped in front of a fish tank
and told me to choose lunch.
You looked gutted when I baulked
and I regret that now, of course.
But you happily picked a spider crab,
and the four of us ate.
Sea, saltiness, calvados . . .
Walking later, my shoes full of sand
and my stomach crabmeat,
I saw more of the dead –
sifted onto the beach by the tide,
cold and sodden and still.

Grève de Lecq

On the beach the trash of living things.
Shells and Styrofoam and packets of sugar.
I stand there, up to my knees –
deep as I dare go out of my element,
and watch a gannet dive for fish.
The bay is named in a foreign language
and the birds are unfamiliar.
Bodies do not wash up here
but show themselves at their leisure.
Of course I don't turn down
the opportunity to spend my money.
Two beers please. And a bowl
of water for the dogs.

The Grey Headlands

Green lizards sunned themselves
on the tennis court of the abandoned chalet
with its almost-French name.
Gatekeepers hid themselves in the dying grasses.
Like the ground, the butterflies were dust –
on this island the soil is suffering its own crisis.
The steep fields had once more offered up
their customary, well-protected crop.
Before the end we would beg for rain,
having long forgotten
the words for the relevant gods.

The Lost Manor at St Marie

It's true that not all life taxes itself
with a sense of scale.
That these buried things below the sand
show themselves as breath –
holes in the beach beneath the waves
that arrive
       and depart in one motion.

There is a manor with the same name as you,
with the small addition of sainthood,
marked *Engulfed by the ocean, 1306.*
An impossible end to settlement
so far gone it had become atlantic.

Didn't it rain . . . and when the rain came,
fine, finally, I remembered the singing.
And the goats –
at the foot of the sloped field of wild flowers –
running for the cover of corrugated iron.

Photograph of Chet Baker

A face like penance
or perhaps just somebody looking down
at the keys of a piano.
Most things appear twice,
but not the piano hinge of course.
The face, the hair – justifiably so.
But the matinee idol looks
always alluded to something not quite him.
Something to escape from.
A trumpet player who sang,
a singer who played trumpet –
he had two sets of front teeth,
the first ruined in a fight
along with his embouchure.
The next, a denture, built to last.
The years in Europe,
a home-from-home.
A classic second act –
the trumpets on *Shipbuilding*
and *Live at Ronnie Scott's*.
A new generation, another bite
(not at art, but at a career).
A film of his life that wasn't his life.
In Amsterdam he fell out of a window.
The police report states
that the two substances found in his room
were also found in his body.

Belleville

(for Yann Le Marec)

Leftist, hilly, just dirty enough.
An apartment with all its perfect stuff.
The old Jean Prouvé chairs,
the old French kitchen utensils,
the old Brêton work clothes.
Old meant good, and not necessarily valuable.
Nothing in the place meant nothing.
Uncomfortable, very cool. Cold, even.
It roused suspicion in us
that nobody around there ever 'stayed in'
(all the young people sat outside the bars . . .).
Do I recall that we were sold on the views?
Chinese restaurants, supermarkets, fireworks.
Chinese New Year and Chinese prostitutes
whose New Balance shoes
all had the 'N' the wrong way round.
Displaced parakeets in the Parc de Belleville.
North-African grocers, Lebanese sandwiches, Tunisian Jews.
Over there now, you tell me,
the boulevards have bloomed gilet jaunes.

The Paris—Texas Crossroads

Nights spent drinking and fumbling around
with funny money. Running through idioms with our
   French host,
a Texan country singer and that friend of his —
the pair of them from the same town
and both with the same name.
The country singer was on his second life
he said — no booze, this time, no strife.

He took us to a crêpe place
where he had been put up
once between record deals
and had played for dinners and drinks.
The batter was as good as the music
and we drank small cups of Brêton cider
which reminded you of home.

You were running from the salt-lick
of your island life, you told us later,
while we went through beer after beer
under the plastic covers outside a street-corner bar.
We compared dead teeth — front left
and ruined by brothers at the same age.

Towards morning, and hungry again,
we walked past Dirty Dicks
and looked in at the window —
Ah J . . .
the girls have all gone now

and the place is a Tiki bar.
I still think about the obscured faces
in the dark looking out at us.

I have been in a couple of times since
and ordered my usual Old Fashioned.

All Over Everything

Sugar money, drug money.
Blood money, oil money, man money.
Mattress money, spun money.
Serious money. Silly money.
Pharmaceutical and avocado money.
Easy money . . .

Two ravens on the edge of a sink left out
by an old barn.

They wouldn't know or care —
they wouldn't think or remember.

February

I could forget it all on evenings like this –
the names, addresses, even our relations.
Everything could be taken
by the lights of the town in this weather.
The process has something to do with the buildings –
their vernacular of flint and brick,
but there is also the matter of the people.
How many there are . . . do we know? Can we trust
    the data?
The dogs at the borders, lapping it up,
must surely just have their own reasons.
And there are dogs wherever a line is drawn.
The map on my phone tells me (not just location)
but that I am quarter of an hour from a drink.
And that is all the news I can handle.

The World's First Ghost

(i.m. Jason Molina 1973–2013)

We only had a handful of nights
in his last handful of months in the country.
I supposed he was broke
so I bought a box of his old CDs
(was that help?) for the record shop
where I worked at the time.
There were some agitated phone calls
(lots of Warren Zevon talk),
some scotched plans to meet up.
A gig or two, a couple of daytime beers.
And then gifts like that firework,
the Merle Haggard Songbook,
an old Pendleton shirt
(still unworn – after all, he stood five six . . .),
a favourite book of poems (Marvin Bell).
I heard from his record label
he'd had to move home,
whatever, wherever, that meant by then.
Perhaps a place where he wouldn't fall over himself.
Or if he did, could land on softer soil.
The land of the nothing-for-free –
certainly not medication, not security.
O Grace!, he sang.

Brown Trout in Zion

We suffered that first desert night.
Bourbon and a bucketful of hotel ice.
Model military jets hung behind the bar,
a photo of a young man in uniform.
The cowboy hats shot us a look
when we ordered Mexican beer.

God bless the fishes of the canyon country –
all that sweet, pink flesh we ate.
And that little horse they gave me,
Bob, who was so short and fat
that when I sat on top of him to ride
my feet were practically on the ground.

Hasher County

Okie From Muskogee on the jukebox.
Your choice, I recall.
A sign in the bar welcomes us
to 'the town that marijuana built.'
This *is* Haggard country, a man says.
They were green for your accent.
Out of the truck window the next day,
more of Merle on the radio,
it was as if the deep verdancy
of the trees either side of the road
reached all the way back to England.
All the way south to Peru.

America Ground

Truthfully speaking what can I offer
her here, in her own country?
The night before last
I took her to some strip bar
with a second-rate male model friend.
The first one wouldn't let us in —
gentlemen only they said.
So we moved on until we found a place.
There had been drowned towns
back home, I told her, this summer.
That bit by the coast that washed up whole
as stone and silt and pebbles after storms,
and where church bells still ring out from the sea
and every few paces fish heads
or the thick mid-sections of skate,
un-winged by gulls and jackdaws
crop up on the suburban bank
of false, impermanent land.

Hurricane Season

The tops of the palm trees
cropped by a coalition of local woodpeckers
and bad weather – the season's getting longer every year.
Seven black seabirds
(unmistakeable, large, tail-shape diagnostic)
above me for what feels like days.
I saw a man who'd lost both legs and one arm
disappearing into the sea to swim.
I stood in the doorway, quiet, waiting for you to dress.
To put on make-up and jewellery.
When we ate, I drank bottles of expensive beer
from Europe, almost as strong as wine.
I was dead tired by ten each night, every night.

A Summer of Seaweed

Brown pelican mornings —
regular as the man hawking fruit and veg
off an old flat-bed truck
up and down the only road in town.
It is the highway only here turned small,
into dirt track.

The birds die from hunger —
diving into salt water for a decade or more
turns them prematurely blind.

Countless flies make home
and food in the sargassus
which has washed up overnight along with the plastic,
old white goods, armaments.

Swimming out won't help.
It is a patch of ocean entirely lost to rust,
and the seabirds — migratory, magnificent —
are all born oil-black.

Vulture

One more turkey vulture for the road.
Downed the shot
and felt its talons tearing through my gut.
Take me home, take me home . . .

Mobile Home

Your folks' house was a mobile home
where the guns were fake
and your Dad called my brother 'Chavez'
and pointed them at him
every single time we knocked for you.

Ripping cones in your car
up in the woods as an offering of peace –
the windows down so we could
smell the pine mingled with the weed.

We could hear woodcocks and owls
over the car stereo
and all that American primitive stuff
you insisted on back then.
We would have listened all night
whatever you had played.

Reading Kinky Friedman

Hair of the dog
(beer, tomato juice, Tabasco, ice),
a bit of pedal steel
and I'm back at that bar
with the shuffleboard and tamales.
Reading Kinky Friedman
playing at Sherlock Holmes in New York.
What was it he wrote?
Something about Elvis and Coca-Cola . . .
a bad joke about where to get good Mexican food.
A country song called 'They Don't Make Jews Like Jesus
  Anymore'.

iPhone

Photographs of everything.
Previous perspectives.
An archive of things
I had not known to forget.
Fixed points.
Maps that have logged me
onto old locations.
Updated weathers. Outdated lists.
Clumps of acronymed chatter.
Somewhere, some huge news.
A code of communal despondence.

Thanks, I'll Eat it Here

The baby boomer method.
A dad taking aim with his record collection.
This one's for you and all that.
I took his choice to mean I left more than the usual mess.
Got us both arrested
the previous Christmas, for instance.
Un-mended all manner of fences.
Twenty million other things not done.
There was a day I just stopped working –
and of course there was a 'you'
who was all I could think about.
It's different with a little age,
more calm, less sabotage, less blue.
The same lyrics have us talking
now about Lowell for a boy's name.
If – given all that old chaos – we should still try.

Moth Book

Echoes of myself as dust
in the places I have been
but am no longer. Morning doubts.
The veracity of recollection.
Something half–lit – dimness, gloom.
The frail civility of a glass of water
and painkillers on a bedside table by the moth book.
Discussion at dinner about displacements –
emptyings which have gone unseen.
My leavings that are never quite in peace –
and the thousands that there are,
vanished beyond naming, beyond knowing.

Song for Uncle Dee

My uncle stayed a few days back.
His van and polished boxes –
all that old gear.
He took the boat out over the oyster beds
on Sunday and pulled in three bass.
Like cold babies.
Left two in the fridge for Mum
then struck out for elsewhere, I guess.

Biography

Every impression of a quiet life – steady, long.
A fishing coat and bird book impression.
The workshop at the bottom of the garden,
the pottering, the seedlings needing potting on,
another cricket season
finished in the cold of autumn,
mouthfuls of siskin song.
The war-years and post-war-years – young, alive, strong.
Awkward military school impressions –
something post-colonial, sub-tropical, Indian.
The fundamentally disagreeing about, or with, or on
the wearing of jeans, or your hair too long.
The years of impressing his opinion
whatever it happened upon.
The strangeness of a new generation,
difficulty with computers, suspicion –
the anti-virus, anti-malware obsession.
A late lingering on –
a slight malingering, regression.
Palliative care, fat gut all gone.
The unconvincing conviction
there was life yet to come.
One last bad night. All done.
Those first, earliest impressions –
to who do they belong?
The council flat and dog-piss stained kitchen linoleum,
summers of maggots and the bins they'd overrun.
Somebody else's life spun on –
his life, in short. You just played the part of son.

A Man Made of Water

In the afternoon my father
and I went from the hospital
straight to my grandfather's house.
I hung my coat two pegs
away from his old fishing jacket
and made us coffee.
My grandfather muted
the naval battle on the TV
and asked how his wife was.

        She's the same, Dad.

We sat around together for the first
time that I could remember –
just us, the three men.

On the morning that he died,
it began to rain from almost
the exact moment that my father
called to tell me. And although
this would have been
too sentimental for both their
tastes, I was glad for a man
who more than any of us
was made of the water.

The Word for Wood

All winter I have pursued the flat voice
of my reading. Simple words
have charged themselves against me,
or filled themselves up while I was looking elsewhere.
There is a double sense that things are just
wrong. Or wrongly labelled.
I cannot, for instance, figure out
how the light has thrown my shadow
upside down on the wall
across the river as I walk beneath the bridge.

The fertility symbols of other, older cultures
harass me through the cold wood.
The sounds of jackdaws going berserk
(though the sound is not their name . . .).
I might as well come clean –
all this is to impress somebody else
though they have long given up interest.
First I read they had left the conversation,
then I watched them leave the house,
finally I heard they left town.

Sometimes this place is barely an eco-system,
and I am just another walker
in the landscape. A golfer who has got lost
and is wearing the wrong jacket.
Of course there is a section in darkness.

Let's call it the late middle. Perhaps the middle eight.
Your dogs have wandered off the path –
followed their innate memories of the pack
into the wood. The howls are maddening.

Heavy Weather

The noise that cracked us open
was two or three miniature motorcycles,
a noise from out of doors –
like the bees I had read were dying.

There were rubber boats in the news
and no borders to heavy weather
wherever you were.
And those few weeks after your birthday –
the last of summer –
was when the bone-cold came on.

They said it would come, a rain like this.
We're up late
with one of your coughing fits.

A good job
the morning has nothing
but its stale name, the non-echo of night.
No work anymore, no tasks.

Acknowledgements

Thanks to the editors of the following publications where versions of these poems first appeared: *Ambit, Elementum, Elsewhere Journal, The New European, Five Dials*, Caught by the River.

Thanks to Declan Ryan, Andrew McNeillie, André Naffis-Sahely, Robert Selby, Lavinia Greenlaw, Julia Copus, Jeff Barrett, Diva Harris and everyone at Caught by the River, Danny Mitchell, Carl Gosling, Kirsteen McNish, Hannah Peel, Erland Cooper, Anna Fidalgo Kelly, Becky Thomas.

Special thanks to Martha Sprackland.

Love and thanks to Mum and Dad, Adam Killip, Steve Blackwell, Greg Burns (the boys in the band), the regulars at The King and Queen, and most especially to Nina Hervé for her love, support and forbearance.

The title 'Kindness, I Suppose' is taken from the Townes Van Zandt song, 'Pancho and Lefty'.

The title 'Thanks, I'll Eat it Here' is borrowed from Lowell George's solo album from 1979.

The title 'The World's First Ghost' is taken from the Magnolia Electric Co song 'O! Grace'.